Marketing Your Business with Social Media Strategies

Diane Winbush

ISBN-13:

978-1523889556

ISBN-10:

1523889551

Photo Illustrations by Gerd Altmann & Ralph Nas

What is Social Media?

Social media are computer-mediated tools that allow people or companies to create, share, or exchange information, career interests, ideas, and pictures/videos in virtual communities and networks.

Social media is defined as "a group of Internet-based applications that build on the ideological and technological foundations of Web 2.0, and that allow the creation and exchange of user-generated content."

Furthermore, social media depend on mobile and web-based technologies to create highly interactive platforms through which individuals and communities share, co-create, discuss, and modify user-generated content.

They introduce substantial and pervasive changes to communication between businesses, organizations, communities, and individuals.
These changes are the focus of the emerging field of techno self-studies. Social media differ from traditional or industrial media in many ways, including quality, reach, frequency, usability, immediacy, and permanence.

Social media operate in a dialogic transmission system (many sources to many receivers). This contrasts with traditional media that operates under a monologue transmission model (one source to many receivers).

"Social media has been broadly defined to refer to 'the many relatively inexpensive and widely accessible electronic tools that enable anyone to publish and access information, collaborate on a common effort, or build relationships."

There are many effects that stem from Internet usage.

Internet users continue to spend more time with social media sites than any other type of site.

"At the same time, the total time spent on social media in the U.S. across PC and mobile devices increased by 99 percent to 121 billion minutes in July 2012 compared to 66 billion minutes in July 2011."

Our company became knowledgeable of social media in 2012. There was much fear due to personal information being shared. As I learned more and more about the platforms; I was able to set privacy setting into place to protect our identity.

Is it important to protect your personal business information on social media? Yes, because you don't want to become a target for unwanted junk mail.

Social Media

We continue to grow with this trend of social platforms but utilize them in a reasonable time frame. It is important that we are not consumed each day about marketing and advertising on social media.

We are to use time wise efforts in marketing to have a productive day in other ways for business.

Time Wise Management

As mentioned in the previous segment of this book; we shared how important it is to use your time wisely on social media. There are so many opportunities/stories/ and feeds on social media which can attract the eye.

We can lose an entire day by reading other posts and or searching for potential business pitches. We are to search ways of how to manage our time on the platform and remain on that goal.

I remember becoming so drained at times that I would need to take a break from the social platforms. I became worried that if I wasn't on social media that our business wouldn't grow or that we were missing potential clients by not searching the feed.

I created two groups for business and inspiration and there was little feedback on the business side.

This exhausted me for months. I desired to know what I was doing wrong the reason why the group was giving little feedback. I also was a radio show host as well as a marketing pitch for business and planning marketing events in our location to help brand the business.

I was worn out. I decided one day to exit social media as an individual for business, but as a paid entity. Once you become a paid entity, the social platforms will do the rest of the work for you online.

You can set your own price range and location of advertising. I knew that my business would fall if I wasn't on social media all day.

We must trust the fact that social media isn't the only tool in which we can use for marketing. What about before time when social media wasn't heard of?

How did entrepreneurs and CEO's win for success back then? Social Media just arrived to make the business flow and operate more frequent and smoother for businesses.

But there are additional ways to market and advertise such as a radio show, book, monogram t-shirt or sweater, create a website, newsletters, television ads, newspaper ads, build-board ads, and more.

Although we feel that these are dated and ancient ways to build and market a business; but it also has more options for the entrepreneur instead of placing all your "eggs into one basket."

So, here's what *Kevan Lee* has to say from *Buffer Social*. "Social media management can be a full-time job, and even for those who do social along with any number of other tasks, social media marketing can still take 10 or more hours every week."
So, what would you do if you only had 30 minutes to spend on social media?

How would you prioritize your tasks, so you make the absolute most of your valuable time?

I tend to find pockets of time throughout the day where I wish I could be as productive as possible in windows here and there.

When a 30-minute window opens, what should I be doing to maximize my time on social media?

Here are some ways I've attempted to use my 30-minute chunks, and maybe they'll spark some ideas for your marketing spurts as well. I'd love to hear what solutions you've found, too!

A study by *Ipsos* found that the average social network user spends 3.6 hours on social media every day.

Considering you may only be awake for 16 hours each day, that means nearly 25 percent of our waking time is spent on Facebook, Twitter, and the rest.

The age breakdown shows the average daily use for younger social media users is even higher.

• 4.2 hours per day – age 35 and under
• 3.1 hours per day – 35-49-year-olds
• 2.8 hours per day – age 50 and over

Wow! Thirty minutes per day in social media marketing suddenly seems quite small.

The daily tasks of a social media manager. Social media managers do not sit around playing on Facebook all day. They have a schedule crammed full of activities and tasks and to-dos.

In our post about social media managers, we identified 12 elements of their job that get handled daily.

As you can see from these articles, that social media can be time consuming. We must set a schedule as to when we are accessing the social media platforms.

They are quite engaging and interesting, but your time is valuable for you and others around you.

Social Media

We all feel that we are going to miss something if we aren't on social media. With a paid app and or account; this can free up much of your time.

Paid Ads with Social Media

Paid advertising allows you to submit your target, your daily budget amount, and the description of your ad. The rest is up to your social platform. If you are a paid client on social media; there is no need for you to linger on these platforms all day.

Once you submit and create your ad, then you can free up your time and allow the big guys to do the work for you. If you are going to market while they are marketing for you then the effort is meaningless.

As I shared earlier, our business created groups and pages, but very little response. They weren't paid accounts. Once the business began to grow and I no longer desires to appear on social media as seeking potential clients; I rested with the fact that our job is done.

Social media will do the rest for us while we are flexible on other things for the business.

Facebook and LinkedIn are two great social platforms which can reach many targets for your business. It allows you to set your daily budget, your target location you would like to reach, description of your product and services, and more.

Other social platforms offer advertising opportunities as well, but these two are a great fit for professionals whom are looking for growth.

You as the owner should strategically plan this out so that you can put some worries behind you.

According to *Evan LePage of Hoot Suite*; he states that "Last year, internet advertising surpassed newspaper advertising spending for the first time."

Advertisers spent $5.1 billion on social media advertising in 2013 and this figure is expected to exceed $14 billion by 2018."

In the third quarter of 2014, Facebook brought in $2.96 billion in advertising revenue, 66 percent of which came from mobile ads.

Twitter generated 85% of its total revenue from mobile advertising in the same quarter, representing about $320 million.

Still not convinced of the value of social ads?

On Facebook, desktop ads have 8.1x higher click-through rates and mobile ads have 9.1x higher click-through rates than normal web ads.

Meanwhile, Promoted Tweets have shown average engagement rates of 1-3 percent— much higher than traditional banner ads.

It's no wonder that by June of this year, nearly 80% of US marketers were using promoted Tweets.

Social media advertising isn't just a buzzword anymore. It's a real, tangible driver of leads and sales, and marketing departments are increasing their social ad spend across the board in response.

Facebook, Twitter and other social networks are filled with hundreds of millions of consumers."

As you can see once again, social media has climbed the ladder in sales for advertising. Many times, we are impatient for replies and responses. We pay a certain amount for our ads and we are seeking a quick reply.

There may be times which you may have need to spend a little to receive more. If this will be your first ad, you must know that it takes a minute to build, brand, market, advertise, and get results.

Your results will show when you have put in the hard work and efforts of building your empire. Just as it may take weeks or months for a baby learn to walk; it will take time for your business to grow and receive exposure. Another marketing you can use for visibility is Build Board (marquis) ads.

These will be much more expensive, but you will receive the results that you are seeking if the customers are interested or targeted for your product and services. Whether you receive a call, a client booking, a referral or not; you just continue to strive for more.

That's the purpose of branding. You must continue to move forward although you haven't received any responses. You can easily fell that you are not where you should be; but you are. It's just taking time to get your market to where it should be.

And this is what you are seeking. You shouldn't desire to be the top of the line and haven't put in any "sweat & tears" for your business.

How can you have a testimony without a story or struggle of getting to your limit or target. This causes other entrepreneurs and business professionals to mimic others.

If you have a desire to mimic others or copyright another's' diligent work; you will not be in business long. Why? Because you are building from another individuals' mission, vision, and purpose.

You may have all your I's and T's crossed and dotted. But at the end of the day; you will not win. You will carry someone else's victory without the testimony and later it will begin to show.

For example: Susie attended college to become a business coach. She had to save for gas and food to maintain for school and some leisure. Susie's vehicle wasn't the best of condition and she rarely had gas to put in her gas tank.

She would remain on campus to live in the dormitory so that she wouldn't place strain on her parents' income.

She worked a part time job to pay for extra material which she needed for upcoming classes. She wanted to remain ahead.

This was the reason why she prepared for the journey. All her colleagues would go out on the weekend shopping and hanging out, but Susie couldn't because she had to remain focus on her goals for accomplishment.

It was finally four years later and graduation day. Her parents traveled from Alabama to Washington to see her walk the line so to speak. Susie was very happy that she had finally arrived at their destination.

While she sat there with her classmates in the auditorium and waiting for the services to begin; she began to reflect on the struggles which she had faced during her journey.

She recalled the nights which she had to remain up late at night to study for courses and test while her friends were out, how she had to save her money from her part-time job to pay for extra projects for extra credit, how she desired to go shopping with her friends, but she had to save for fuel from work back to school.

She felt that those days were all worth the struggle. See if you cannot be grateful for the struggles, there will never be victory!

Susie began to sigh with relief as she walked to the podium as her name was called out for receiving the Valedictorian award for her college year. You can appreciate more from your hard work than receiving all things with no sweat and tears.

Targeting is Everything

Do you find yourself all over the place? What I mean by this is we can post personal, business, activities, family reunions and much more on our social media links.

If we are branding and marketing for business, we should remain with one pitch for success.

On-lookers can become irritated or confused of who you are. I train professional women monthly regarding our association and the targets which we have for women.

This was one of my phrases which I gave them on our *Professional Women Financial Brunch.*

I advised them that if they are posting personal and business feed, the clients will never know who they are.

Lets' Explore This:

Tammy is marketing her business to brand insurance clientele. Tammy has just posted on her timeline about her parents were visiting from Florida.

She goes on to say that she was happy that they were arriving because she hadn't seen them in five years.

This feed posted immediately to her timeline. She returns to her social platforms 4 hours later to remind her friends of her webinar that she is having as a marketing pitch.

She posts 5 hours later that she has felt sick and need her friends to pray for her that she feels better.

Do you see what Tammy has done? How could Tammy have handled this in a different way?

_____

_____

_____

_____

_____

_____

_____

_____

_____

_____

_____

_____

_____

_____

_____

Tammy has created an environment which her potential clients are not sure who she is.

She has posted different things and each post was not the same. If you need prayer, you should go to your local dioceses, or clergy for prayer. Leave this out of your commenting if you are marketing on social media.

If family is spending time with you, and we know this is a joyful event; but we must not forget that why we are on social media as business owners.

Have you ever heard the old saying; *"Never mix business with pleasure."*

We should remain on one topic and one focus to market effectively. When creating a page; you will have the option to select your region or location as to where you desire to reach your target. Facebook will provide tons of choices for you to make your business visible.

We have a virtual office in Florida and this is a great tool for marketing in your targeted location.
Here are some more facts which can help you in marketing with targeting for your audience by *Evan Le Page of Hoot Suite:*

1. Use free social media to beta-test your paid social ads

You're likely already sending out multiple Tweets, Facebook Posts and LinkedIn Updates every day. Some of these messages will resonate with followers; others won't. Track which ones are being clicked, shared and commented on. These high-performing messages make the best candidates for native social ads.

2. Take advantage of targeting features

One of the major issues with traditional ads is inefficiency. Twitter, LinkedIn, Facebook and other social media advertising platforms offer very effective targeting capabilities to address that problem.

From targeting social media managers on LinkedIn to Game of Thrones fans on Facebook, take advantage of this very useful targeting for more efficiency in advertising.

3. *Rotate ads frequently*

One of the biggest issues advertisers deal with on Facebook is ad fatigue. This means, when people start to see your ad too many times, they get bored of it and stop clicking.

Unfortunately, when your click through rate starts to drop Facebook penalizes you, driving up your cost per click (CPC), and making likes, comments, and click through more expensive.

This affects both acquisition and engagement campaigns. A best practice that we use at *Hootsuite* to combat this, is to rotate our ads every 3 to 5 days to keep our content fresh and engaging.

4. Use small samples to A/B test your social ads.

One of the great virtues of social ads is instant feedback. You can gauge the effectiveness of a sponsored post in minutes, and follow up with advanced analytics reports.
With all this available data, you should be sending out several "test" ads to small audiences, tracking the results, and then pushing winning ads to larger groups. It's cheaper and more effective.

5. Understand how ads are sold.

Different networks sell ads in different ways. On Twitter, companies pay on an engagement basis.

Facebook and LinkedIn offer the option of paying per impression. It's critical to design Tweets and Posts accordingly.

For example, since we pay Twitter each time users click on our ads, it's important that people be genuinely interested in the content on the other side.

The goal here is to drive genuine prospects to our site, not merely to attract views.

6. Design your ads with smartphones in mind.

Social media is consumed overwhelmingly on mobile devices. Twitter users spend 86 percent of their time on the service on mobile.

Facebook users aren't far behind at 68 percent. This means most social media ads are being viewed on mobile devices, as well.

As a result, messages must be optimized for viewing on small mobile screens. While this may seem like a pain, Twitter recently unveiled a feature enabling paid Tweets to be targeted by zip code, so it's also a huge advantage.

The main point to keep in mind is to do your homework when advertising and marketing on social media. Make sure that you rad and fully understand your terms and conditions and how much information that social platforms are accessed to. You are on your way to success!

Demographics

Demographics refers to populations, location, gender, ethnic, culture, and more. Merriam-Webster defines demographics as "the statistical characteristics of human populations (such as age or income) used specially to identify markets a change in the state's demographics; a market or segment of the population identified by demographics trying to reach a younger demographic."

Through social media marketing, you can create a structured campaign for your brand.

When I create a marketing campaign through Facebook; many options are offered included a selective price for how much you want to spend. Spending ads for campaigns is important.

Word of mouth is a good way to get the word out about your business. But social millions captivate millions per month.

You don't have to find them, you just must narrow down your demographics, the areas you think your brand will soar, where your customers are and their needs. You can research first as to who needs your product or services before selecting a location.

Research as to what age group would benefit from your brand. Research how many utilize social media and their time frames. Research your target areas' behavior of purchasing your brand and or items like your product.

Research your competitors and what has worked for them in the past according to marketing. You wouldn't have a need to copy their strategy but to get some ideas of what works for them. Set long and short-term goals as to where you see the company/business in the next. Conduct a S.W.O.T analysis on your brand. A *Strengths, Weakness, Opportunities, and Threats* overview will let you know where the brand or product stands.

Summary

Know your pitch for marketing and advertising. Where is my target is what you should be asking or considering? Will I place an ad to an area which possess no growth or interest for your product or for business?

If you are a paid advertiser, you need not to remain on social media throughout the day. The purpose of you promoting your business with a paid ad is to provide leverage for you and the business and you can be flexible for more business opportunities. Let the business process you. Don't expect immediate results and you have only launched your business three years ago. The business will still need nurturing. You are still in your baby steps of a process. Be patient and watch your business excel for excellence.

www.ingramcontent.com/pod-product-compliance
Lightning Source LLC
Chambersburg PA
CBHW050358180526
45159CB00005B/2073